THE SELECTED POEMS
OF HOWARD McCORD
1955 - 1971

Preface by Theodore Enslin

The Crossing Press, Trumansburg, New York 14886

ACKNOWLEDGMENTS

Poems in this volume are selected from
PRECISE FRAGMENTS, Dolmen Press, 1963
12 BONES, Goosetree Press, 1964
THE SPANISH DARK, Wash.State U. Press, 1965
FABLES AND TRANSFIGURATIONS, Kayak, 1967
LONGJAUNES HIS PERIPLUS, Kayak, 1968
THE FIRE VISIONS, Twowindows Press, 1970
MAPS, Kayak, 1971

The author is grateful to the editors of the many magazines
in which these poems first appeared.

Designer/illustrator: Harley Elliott

Photo of the author: Colman McCord

THE CROSSING PRESS SERIES OF SELECTED POETS

This project is supported by a grant from the National Endowment
for the Arts in Washington, D.C., a Federal agency.

Library of Congress Cataloging in Publication Data

McCord, Howard, 1932-
     The selected poems of Howard McCord, 1955—1971.

     (Crossing Press Series of Selected Poets)
     Bibliography: p.
     I. Title.
PS3563.A263A6 1975   811'.5'4   75-5701
ISBN 0-912278-56-0
ISBN 0-912278-57-9 pbk.
ISBN 0-912278-65-X lim. ed.

A frightening thing, when a man decides to collect or select poems which have meant much to him at various periods in his life. A frightening thing to gather together any other parts. There is the embarassment at times, in remembrance, and the hopelessness in front of certain achievements which one may never be able to go beyond. And above all, there is the feeling of disjointedness which comes from the attempt to straddle back: You cannot share what you are with what you were. I think it is best to say this first, because in this book it is evident that McCord realized these things, went at his work with fear and trembling, and produced something which shows few of those agonizing scars. There is little here for him to wince at. He makes a homogenous whole out of nearly twenty years of concern. The young man climbing mountains, alone in deserts—feeding and drinking, starving, and thirsty—and what I like most of all, a whole man who is in and out of doors. Concerns for books and learning (never the pretense or show of it), a religious man who does not prate or presume to tell anyone else where the road lies, and finally a fine craftsman. It would be presumptuous of me to take more of his time. It is a big book, and a good one. A book I will treasure.

Theodore Enslin

CONTENTS

INTRODUCTION

As a poet, I've not been very concerned with defining the poem, or articulating an esthetic that coherently relates the poem to my life and my culture. When some small *click* of satisfaction and surprise emerges from the shape of words on the page I am happy enough, and take it as a signal to move on to the next poem. As a teacher and sometime critic, however, I have been forced to think out and express (always inadequately) what I think the poem is and does, and what it's good for.

I hold the poem is mutant information, delirious, proper as a geometry, antidote to common reason, heart-honest, an earthly echo of the continuous feasting of angels. It is the celebration which confirms joy and uncertainty in us. It keeps our tongue supple and our eyes bright. It is a necessary foolishness for me, who must pray daily or not think at all.

The landscape of my poems is language, but tempered by a special love for wilderness and a dedication to walking. Certain mountain ranges and empty spaces -- The Organs, close by Las Cruces, New Mexico, the Chiracahuas, the Jarbidge Range, the Steens, the Wallowas, the central highlands of Iceland, Kebnekaise massif in Lapland, the Crags in the Selway-Bitterroot, Hueco Tanks, the Guadalupes, the Franklins, the foothills of the Himalayas, the Western Ghats, even the little hills in which Mycenae sits -- have been places in which I have felt an energy focus on me, and that energy clarify me, and reveal itself in poems. Mountains, deserts, and the sea, like physics, present me with orders outside myself which I must accommodate, and thereby grow.

Wilderness and solitude are often the theaters in which the poems occur, but the human concerns are linked to the loving and intricate relationships I have been graced with and value more than the wildest geography. It is my wife, Dora, my sons, Robert and Colman, all my family, and the many friends over the years who have helped me understand, set me puzzles, loved and put up with me, and given me the rudiments of what decency I can claim. This book is for me a celebration of many years, and I do not feel that it is an indulgence to thank some of them here: Robert and Joy Sterling, Lafayette and Bethel Young, Geoffrey Young and Laura Chester, Haldeen Braddy, Howard Sherman, Dan Vickers, David Burwell, Gordon Curtis, Ammon Hennacy, Walter Lowenfels, Siv Cedering Fox, Cheryl Doering, George Hitchcock, Henry Grosshans, Dan and Pat McLachlan, Gus Blaisdell, Keith Wilson, Ted Enslin, and Randall Ackley.

The rest is said by the poems.

Howard McCord

A DAY'S JOURNEY WITH GEOFFREY YOUNG

pictographs

1)   and at the river
     a shape traced on a stone
        the cull of a shape
        by a degenerate hand
     The Shoshoni no Chichimecs

     rude, inglorious, a fish-stink
        heavy as fog.

     No castaway Phoenicians, lost navigators
     Shoshoni and brute, illiterate

     But they danced and knew
        the orgasm
     and ate every day they could.

2)   the road to Billy Meadows
        is hardly there anymore

     Buckhorn Creek splits
     and the map doesn't know where anybody is.

     The canyon
     so far and lonely and deep
     exactly

        flight
        and the hands of God

        Bless us
        keep us safe from harm.

3)   small campsites
       a rabbit femur, some charcoal,
       hardly out of the wind
       They called them the "grass-house people"
       and Bonneville found them "wintering in such shelters
                         without roofs, being merely
                         half circles of brush, behind
                         which they obtained but an imperfect
                         protection"

       But this is Nez Perce,
             Sahaptin country,
       the Shoshoni far upstream
       with an "imperfect protection"

the fall

4)   Licentious, vulgar greed
       and the white skin of Satan are not new
       and if Viet Nam is unspeakable
       its total antecedent
       is (in this local space)

                The Treaty of 1855
                violated by the Treaty of 1863
                (the white shits had found gold in the Wallowas)
                and the vicious exile 1877-1904
                of Joseph

       Nature's gentleman, the ladies could say
       (who would not suffer a black hand inside their thighs)
       a retreat worthy of Xenophon
                "incommoded with women & children"
       but the morality of law is power.

5)   here the road
        breaks off the crest
               and we've never got to a single place
               any sign said was coming up

The lesson of history, precisely.

               As Standing Bear was denied
               writ of habeas corpus because
               he was not a "person within
               the meaning of the law."
               Reversed 18 April 1877
               but who believed?

the road forks again
and down the one
we did not take is the Master
(always)

the trees see him ride the sound of his drum
going where the dead are afraid to go
prophesying with a spider on his tongue.

               on our road: chukar, three does
               a broken trestle rot-green with moss
               a flat tire, a sinister man
               with his bones on top of his skin,
               and coming up, rain.

The magic we have is that we do not believe in magic
and will not retreat.

6) the best thing
    would be to go back to the crest

            camp

    then wait and see what the dawn
    is like from the very top.
    Away from the damned white man
    and the war
    left with just the bones of Indians
    wind
    & the music in your head.

            "The exact nature of Indian
            ownership of land
            appears not to have been understood
            by the early settlers, and the
            misunderstanding was the fruitful source
            of trouble and even bloodshed."

    There is no way back,
            only the disease of our history
            the mutilation of land,
            murder

    The Skidi Pawnee gave up a woman to the morning star
    about corn-planting time

    but not every year.

            Our way is the ten o'clock napalm
            absolute possession
            a percentage
            treachery

    "General Jessup, maddened by the public cry
    for more energetic action, seized Osceola
    and his attendants while holding a conference
    under a flag of truce."

    beyond

7) The best thing
   would be to sit on the ridge
   wrapped in a Chilkat blanket
   and watch everything go away.

              lies
              Zyklon-B and C S gas
              the constabulary of Grenada, Mississippi
              the torture of children
              Lidice and My Lai
              Wounded Knee, Hue,
              Sand Creek, all
              of Quang Ngai Province.

8) We have yet to comprehend
   the pilgrimage of Smohalla, prophet
   and wanderer of the Sokulk

              "he left home secretly
              and absented himself for a long time"

On foot to Mexico about 1850
back through Nevada and the spirit land

       messages
          : :give up the white man: :
   return to trees and stone
   and the Dream.

But he knew this country
we look at, Geoff,
and he knew the death that was coming to it
would never go away.

THE MONTHS OF THE TRIBE

for Lafe

The goat month, when piñones are gathered.
The month of barren horses.
There is the month of persimmons
    and it is permitted to be bitter.
    The grandmothers wail
    and husbands are chastised.
Orion at dusk marks the time
    when fields are planted
    and the sweet cunts of women
    are moist as peaches.
    Then the penis of a man is swollen
    and heavy, hanging like a thick cord
    that runs from his belly to his heart.
The best month to gather wood comes
    two moon-deaths after harvest.
    The sap has fled, but the cold
    does not yet bruise the fingers.
Some years there is a month, deep in winter,
    when a man does nothing
    but curse and drink.
Before the last snow clears young men
    are sent out to endure
    and young women are shown
    the secrets of coupling. They dance.
In the month of chaos the earth is killed
    and men riot to bring it to life.
    A wild month, full of pain and noise
    and finally joy.

THE TOAD MAN

a poem for Stob

I

I say
endure the law of things,
the wasted joke of the night.
Walk away.

>In the forest the needles
>of the larch are loosening,
>a yellow pale as white alder leaves

The rains have come, half snow,
and the brush is heavy and cold
in the gray shadows

My pants are wet through
in a hundred yards
and a chill works up my back
before I sweat.

>Six miles on the logging road,
>two miles along the ridge.

Two miles is just far enough
to pack a rocking chair.

I made the shack, what Kephart
calls an "axeman's cabin"
eight by ten, but with a borrowed
chain-saw the butterflies out
>tumbling in the first hot weather.

Brought in a welded metal stove,
that rocking chair.

I stay there
to endure

the delight
the defeat.

II

My pleasures
are in solitude, a fire,
my own plain cooking,
the prayer of the wind.

I must wander both beneath and upon the earth
a herdsman and gatherer of sycamore fruit

> I can sing any song whatever,
> for any time
> because the waters flow eternally

(the truth of sage, marjoram,
> basil, the wine of the condemned,
> the plumb line
> and the quarrels of men)

There is no order.
Neither in reed
> nor flint
> nor the house of the sun
> nor the rabbit
nor in the blessings of gentility.

I tell you there are only
> the myths of childhood
geometry
nothing more.

III

I drink whisky some,
smoke grass, and have
a hot water bottle.

> Tuck that in the bedroll
> on a cold night
> and it's all right.

They kill out there

> I paint, read books, hear
> the toads call from the spring,
and wait, my heart like a locust.

Summer comes
and I start the garden
watch after the hives

> eight
> beehives at the edge of the meadow

They always get through the winter

They've got secret ways of staying warm, like toads --

> they never die.

LEARNING

Reading one column of Chinese
slowly as paralysis
with dimmed understanding

hunting among the strokes
for a root shape
that traps meaning

my eyes tense and hurting
with the new task
I breathe slowly

as though the characters
were ash a breath
could spoil.

Nothing in the West
is so silent, lips
stiff and frozen,
but mountains
and the blooming of flowers
- -- trillium, oxeye daisy,
Drummond's anemone.

THE SPIRIT DREAM

for Rob

I

Eight big sticks
        all I could find
without going back too far
and I wanted to sit the night
out on top.

I was thirteen
musette bag with 2 oranges
can of Dinty Moore stew
a copper bowl
dried apricots & oatmeal
Canteen and a great knife
on a belt, knife too big
but stout as hell
        -- I've still got it --
probably split rock.

Army blanket.

        Franklin Peak, the old tin
        mines to the left, the lights
        of El Paso south
        on both sides of the spine.

It is summer 1945
a full moon is coming like the calendar said

and I am waiting for the spirit dream.

I taught myself all of this,
it is from the books

        but I believe.

I start the fire
keep it small, and face
an implacable, mindless moon
that floats in the waters beyond the firmament.
I have the blanket around my shoulders,
lean against the rock, and spear
chunks of meat from the can
with my big knife.

I catch the moon in the bowl of water,
and shift the universe with my unsteadiness.
I stare, the fire goes to the end,
and as I have planned, I am tired
and fall asleep
into the casting of the flower.

The act and the secret
is to live the vision
to stop in holy infancy
to be imprisoned beneath
      the incorruptible surface
   of the dream.

The gods outside, thick as lice,
speak to my eyes
and I am afraid.

      A cave or a stope, sinister.
      I am going to be left there.
      Then steep, steep hillsides,
      trails, a high fastness,
      trying to find a particular place
         an old ranch house
            horseback
               a paint.

Heavy sacks of sand. Maybe wool.
Sheep with bloody sides
nicked in shearing.

> The cavern is huge. I watch
> lights a quarter-mile down,
> a babbling procession that
> mustn't find us. We slip away
> through heavy brush.

III

I wake to the moon pressing
on my eyelids from the west.
The fire is out, the bowl spilt,
the stars where the moon rose
are back again.

I am thirsty, take up the canteen,
drink, curl in the blanket, and sleep.

Next day
I know my animal is the paint horse
that I must fear men
be always in the fastness.

There is no one to tell this to.

FABLES & TRANSFIGURATIONS

After An Autobiography

I

I drink wine, and the sunshine
off the snow breaks across my eyes
in a tumult of colors,
and the snow, like withers
stung by flies, shivers
in relief: the mind is all horses
whirling in the snow, and wolves
hidden in the shadow of the larch.

I have seen wolves take the weaker
caribou and wring their souls out
on the snow. Not many have seen this,
but souls are white like snow
and full. When they burst
they leave red swamps and wolf tracks
in the snow.

It was the summer I was kept untouched,
and swam beyond the kelp beds every day,
the salt tempting my lips,
the spindrift like thick and rheumy snow.
Far out at sea I'd shout
because I had not spoken for a week
and dive as far into the green
as my lungs reached
where the wolves were clean.

Returning to shore, my body left
to the rocks, a derelict, I
let my eyes empty on the snow
and the stone was colder than the sun.
Far off where my eyes ran
the forest burned and the trees
screamed, chained to the hill.
I stopped my eyes, and read
until the fire went out
and the trees stopped pulling
at their roots. I could not speak.

There were three books: Blake,
Hopkins, Rimbaud. I kept them
wrapped in oilskin with a candle.
Out in the desert, lying by the fire,
I'd light the candle, brood it with my chest,
and read until the moon stopped moving.
The snow was deep and thick upon the sand,
and the four of us were some mad
silent pack whose lips played
with words as if they were lips.

At home, in bed, I coupled Nietzsche
with Saint Paul till both screamed
and one fled. Saint Paul's foolishness
survived: "Every creature of God
is good, and nothing to be refused
if it be received with thanksgiving."
So I praised mountains, and the snow,
and wolves, and slept upon my side
in chains, alone.

It is only historians who think
some events are more important than others,
that a battle is heavier with reality
than a broken gin bottle. Our equality,
however, is that everything is worth nothing.
I have Bowditch on the desk
to find my way, and I plot Sumner lines
and wait neap tides that I may sail
the narrows. I am ignorant, but
the moon hauls at my blood
and the winds are the same everywhere.

At bars in Bangkok, Madras,
Kathmandu, I met three
who smuggled hope as avidly as heroin.
An East Berliner at the Paras Hotel,
a Dane from Vientiane.
The third was a musician in the Carnatic.
Desolate and helpless,
I was on my way somewhere
and bought each of them a beer
and talked awhile.

These go along, as I try and chart
the True Hesperides, with
old service numbers (mine 425-94-25,
Dora's 989-20-95W), empty coordinates
that never found either of us,
two saints: Jude of the impossible,
Dympna of the mad, sons
Robert and Colman.
All of the tribe -- -- maniac shamans
wise in their wounds -- -- Bob, Lafe,
Gordon, Gus, Sam Pendergrast,
the five-two ghost of Fraenkel
I met in the desert
sucking on a rock.

I was always in the desert.
First with a .22, stalking time;
later climbing the rocks in an idiot dance,
the dance of the long fall,
then the solitary, simplistic solution
of the motorcycle wailing at the dunes.

Years back, hunting with peyote,
I hit the bole of a cottonwood tree
and mountains miles away boomed
back against my feet. I beat again
on the thick-fleshed drum and the pebbles
all around the tree danced like rain,
the cottonfields a tambourine
and my horse shouting, raving like a bear.
I rode him five miles at a gallop
then we both fell and rubbed
our faces in the sand. I could not speak.

Time and perception and memory,
an order scalded by life, and the humbug
truth of making it
every day.
Keep confusing the dimensions.
The books.
That's why I need Bowditch,
or Saint Paul.
I'm always right on the edge.

There's this life in me
that's carrying a rifle
and a pack and is off
somewhere -- -- Mexico, the Gobi -- --
and its mind is just intent
on the country. No memories,
no place it's come from,
and just going to the mountains.

I don't even know what language it speaks.

KATHMANDU VALLEY: A HILLSIDE

Tibet is fifty miles away
and the requiem of all that is fugitive
is the low and moaning cry of the wind.
The mountains here break out toward the sky
in a spasm of rock and snow
and hungry villages. Below,
a white stupa covers a relic of Buddha
like cupped hands
and I am very close to walking to Tibet.

It is moving into a falcon's eyes
and brain here on the hillside,
a funny pilgrim rocking on his heels
talking to a brown child
in some tree language of gesture
while out beyond our faces are the Himalayas
and fifty miles away
my cinnamon Tibet.

MY BROTHER'S DEATH

The toxicologist's report:
spittle and rheum
traces of Saint Johnswort
(only poisonous to white-colored animals)
patient was white, originally.

Insisted he drank
infusions of locoweed
(Oxytropis lambertii)
and that salvation
was in antiquity and bone:
not Greek metric

        "Classicism is a sentimentality"

but in olives and wine
and Bronze Age shamans.

The homily was interrupted
by convulsions: when he returned
he quoted the mermaid in *Lighea*

        "I am immortal because
        all the dead things flow into me."

I remember walking down the hill
from Mycenae to the crossroad at Fichtia,
Argos was a blur in the distance
nearly on the gulf
and he had picked some wild garlic
and stuck it in his buttonhole.
We had melon and beer at the crossroad,
with tomatoes, sausage, bread.

"This is the smallest fraud," he said,
gesturing at the food
"and the theater's the key: Silenus
on the tanbark, the hokum of tragedy.
The Romans took it literally and
killed people in the circus, and that's
the west we inherited. The major art
form is death.

That's all. Aristotle and Jeremiah
were never listened to.

No.

Greece gave a value to death,
and the Romans made it
a commodity. Pound and usury
were more right than we admit.
Additionally, the sacraments are true."

The pulse of his voice faltered
and his flesh was yellow as that garlic,
with as rank a smell.
Louis Aragon admitted
Vivre n'est plus qu'un stratageme,
but my brother was not good at winning.

"If you will learn to smelt bronze,"
he said before he died,
"you will be a better philosopher
than the man who knaps flints,
though technology is a pestilence.
Pay attention to the stars
and learn birds' names
as much as anything."

Then he died, a sentimentalist.

We had walked a lot, and once
going up the path to the fortress
at Amber, outside Jaipur,
dodging the piles of elephant shit,
he laughed, and danced a few steps
to the music and

        "Quite naturally," telling
        the wife that left him,
        "I began to cry."

Though we swam at the beach at Nauplia
that night, drank ouzo
and decided to go to Kimolos,
we bred death in actions,
and it was no better than Mahabalipuram
where the sea had been too rough.
It was good, but not enough.

        "What is the velocity reached
        by a falling spider? He can't
        be killed that way.
        He can't fall to his death in air."

Paul's terminal velocity
was zero, anchored in a bed
without a parachute,
his face as yellow as his hair.

YSLETA, TEXAS, 1947

My theology began
with a whistle made of a bird's wing.

Unthinking, I had killed
a buzzard,

> he had settled to the ground
> like a mountain
> in a great exhaustion

and above the stench
had stripped the bones of flesh.

I dried them in the sun,
cut four holes
in the big wing bone

> One for lips
> Three for fingers

The bird was made of death,
with wooden eyes,
and the flute hissed more
like a snake than it sang
and the blowing made me dizzy.

But I was young
and full of nonsense
and thought the dizziness
was to dance to.

I did not know that it was a blasphemy
of death, or that the steps
spelled out I was condemned
and would know fiercer lips
on my own bones before I died.

ALL HALLOWS' EVE

In the motorcycle boots
I bought fourteen years ago
walking down a hillside with Robert,
his two-year old hand tight on a finger
And that afternoon, boots still on,
starting a fire with cedar shavings
at Little Sand Creek
hours and beer later
dousing it, a surplus canvas bucket
1942 I was ten.

On the instep of the right boot
is a gash I got falling off somewhere.
I think in Memphis, a cross-country run
1952, when I bent the forks and blacked an eye.
I had cleat soles put on the boots
in Salt Lake City, 1958, for snow.
Dora and I had a Ford pickup.
Anglo-Saxon, Old Spanish, and Chaucer's
dirty words for thesis. Gave
my foul weather jacket to a beggar man
and never had another. Helped dig a basement.

Colman asks about a trefoil sunset cloud
and sees Venus first.
He talks new all the time, as though he
just came out of blindness
and wants to know the proper names of things.

Robert's gone to sleep in Dora's lap
and there's nothing left of me
that isn't married to her. Nothing but
the old madness, gone now, and maybe
(I was going to say)
these boots, but she's married them, too.
All one flesh in a blue 1960 Fiat
coming into Potlatch, Idaho, 22
miles from home.
Bone of my bone, dreamt and praised.

I was married young, at 20
and was absolutely strayed before it.
I could not apprehend my own numb aimlessness.
I did not know there was any place to be lost in.
That is closer
I did not know there was a place.

The world was simply an extension of my senses
I carried it with me
and it went out when I closed my eyes in sleep.
I had never met anyone I had not invented
until Dora.

                    The curve now of the road
                    through the wheatfields, away
                    from the pine. Colman
                    asks about the dash lights
                    and I name them all,
                    the night going by
                    with a startled look.

At Salt Lake, rock climbing in the Wasatch,
Sanskrit, Matthew Arnold, and I turned
Catholic and stopped getting falling-down
drunk. Bought a .44 Magnum and a .303 Enfield
but I haven't been able to kill anything
since I was seventeen, before I bought the boots.
The motorcycle seemed to take away the need to kill.
Dora was right there with me, going
her way and mine together, somehow,
as she had in El Paso, coming out of the madness,
and in Santa Clara, San Jose, San Diego
when I was in it.
We married in 1953.

        All Hallows' Eve, Kamiak
        Butte is black on the sky and
        when we get to Pullman we'll swing
        up the hill to home. Colman
        is eating an apple, Robert's asleep,
        I'm in the boots
        and so Dora and I hum a bit, on our
        sweet and swinging way to death.

A LETTER OF SAINT ANDREW THE DANCER

i.

Grape, ivy, pine
     fig
          lords of the moist

         myrtle
           (belonging to Dionysus and the dead)

the wet of sex
and the great folds of the sea

The seeds of all
are by nature moist

            Thales no fool

"Does not each one of us
have the face
of one who has died?"

Shiva, lord of sleep, blue-throated,
               whose-form-is-water
      The madness of birth

         Beloved.

ii.

There are exits in the land
Pausanias and the local,
the sense

that in the groundsurge
of high plateaux, in the mute and sleeping
forests

in stone
is the coda of the dance

The markings of birds
and the organic structure
of hieroglyphs
are not distinct

this is the vision Shiva and Dionysus allow

demand

it is the sapience of blood
the demand of bone

spilled in a pattern
cracked on the fire and read

always reading, alert
to the clouds, the direction
of wind, the texture of the soil
the attempt at totality

Shiva and Dionysus allow

demand.

iii.

The Risen Christ consumes

    in the fire

of his burning, motionless body
the dualities
    in great sanity

His sanity

    His sanity is power
    over ecstasy

  the divine madness that is the power

  of Shiva and Dionysus

who are permitted ecstasy and madness

    escape

Only the Risen Christ sanity

    consuming silently
  in a stately, measureless blur of light
unmoving

    quiet

the oppositions, consuming
without movement or action

  the dancing figures of Shiva and Dionysus.

iv.

In the calm of the forest
Christ kills the gods

                     who are the energy of the world
          and the progenitors of birds
                  intelligence
              and the senses

to leave a white, unforgiveable light

        in summation and everywhere

    without distinction
              the still wind of light.

v.

There is no white light but that
      which streams
          from the pine cone

                        thyrsus/lingam

there is no sanity save in madness
and Christ is flesh.

                  Blessed flesh and local, dancing

the world to come
  with such fruit

          and glory of sound

                  the Hosannas

the screams of angels and falcons
      in exaltation,

Mary, Mother of Stars--

the immense dance purified by light
      cleansed of the shadow

                  infinitely expanding

                  (that life may not breed on life again

but all existence
      all alive

infinitely extending in time,

                  the generations
                        the treasures

42

the absolute present consumed and flowering

forever

in the still and moving

wind and light

of Christ.

vi.

Above all

the waters

beyond the firmament

breathe and move

in the restless

and toiling thrust of creation,

lifted and dazzling

and all participate
are of

the silent peace of the white and motionless light
and the contextured grains of earth

the salt and wet

reality

of the sea, the open gates

the dance.

DORA

You have come along with me
looking for the things we lost
and I have found the face
of the human being
in your face.

We are each other's history
and in our magic sleep
steal back the time
that was forfeited with Eden.

We no longer have important fears.

from LONGJAUNES HIS PERIPLUS

LONGJAUNES HIS PERIPLUS

I

A chest of maps
 is a greater legacy
  than a case of whisky.

My father left me both.
 Strong legs, a willingness
  to suffer.

Endurance like the roach, and
 a sense of beauty formed
  by the excellence of geography.

Land was poetry
 and to walk upon it each footstep
  a bird's name

> pipit
> sand piper
> night jar
> kite and jackdaw
> avocet
> godwit
> longspur
> thick-billed murre.

or a stone's.
(I will not name them here).

To hold in my hand a paper
  on which mountain ranges
  islands
    seas

were enumerated
  their contours drawn
  and located
  all rich with the indecision of history
    or what my father said

                    "go along the coast as far as
                    you can without getting killed"

my saint is Hsuan-tsang
  who got back.

To understand the contexts
  of my environment,

                    hieratic
                    costumed
                    even dancing,

demanding to possess the ecology
  of my spirit, the plasm I
  called reality.

Much was denied,

But I was given knowledge of secret places
  in Bhutan, in the Pamirs, a valley running
  to the Turfan depression. Islands.
Given too the species, the particulars
  of coastlines & reefs, caches of stone sculpture,
  what fruits may be eaten without fear.

Once, climbing the Jain rock of
Sravanabelagola, blisters I knew
 to be sacred; once again seeing
  wild elephants move like black flames
   through the forest at Bandipur.

Moonstones as unnerving as ololiuqui
 poured on the table by young Sital Dass
  then turquoise, opals, sapphires, cabochon
  garnets, and amethyst, the stone
   that cures drunkenness.
I listened two afternoons,
 learned what I could, and bought
  a great black stone without a name.

In Varanasi a student of Cannabis
 revealed its variety: sabjee and majoom,
  ganja, bhang, charas,
   Smoke, drunk, made into candy.

            (Majoom, the hemp confection: mix ghee
            with water, add bhang, ganga, charas
            opium, poppy-seeds, dhatura leaves and
            seeds, cloves, mastich, anise seeds, cumin,
            sugar, butter, flour, milk, cardamons,
            and tabashir. Dose one drachm).

All becomes jewel.

The old days in New Mexico,
  the limestone caverns of the Guadalupes,
  the distances of the Tularosa basin.
  Kilburn Hole, Big Hatchet mountains,
    the Peloncillos, all lonely as
      the Chagos of the Indian ocean.
I could walk into the loneliness
I wanted, and fear it.

The displacement of language
  in poetry is as solitary, and as rich
  in the particulars of love,
    of species in time; the simple tune of the equinox,
    all the fires I've seen: pinon, cedar,
      sandalwood, cow shit patties, and tamarack
      spitting like the music at Bodhnath.
        The dead men at the burning ghats.

Coming back home, and waiting.
  Remembering bear skins, camels,
    yaks, horses, bronzes, heavy tents,
    boots, bad water, three
      thousand languages, carts,
        border guards, Mexaform for diarrhea.

My father gave me the freedom of love.
 And with a box of old coins,
  augury by flowers, accounts of the stars
  (Rigel, Algol, Mizar, Aldebaran), a sextant,
   and instruction in the tree of the Sephiroth,
    knowledge that the secrets of Shekinah
    and Tantra are identical, and form
    the full quaternity.
He taught me to walk,
 and rubbed my shins with the fat
  of antelopes.

I knew most what he meant
 when a hundred miles off the coast of China
  I saw the Yellow River still integral,
   holding back the blueness of the sea.

It is for this I walk
 only for this are the many names of birds meaningful.
  Widdershins, the devil's contraries,
   the force of the witch
    exist.
Never believe the law.
 Never obey in conscience: refuse power.

                    Everywhere the solemn
                    malignancy of life
                    is the burden
                    to be carried into the mountains.

I went among simple people.
 In Bhadgaon I sang a madman to defeat.
  He demanded my riches, or cigarettes,
   taunted me in a song, a dark language
    I could only mimic. I sang back at him
    and stopped, ashamed, when my
     jeep driver gave him a cigarette.

Can the murderer know justice?

The singing madman of Bhadgaon --
 my song was a stone.
  Would I give my son a stone?
   But I do not smoke
   I had no cigarettes
    I was frightened.

II

The terebinth, the oaks,
 the sacred grove at Moreh,
  and off to the south the vale of Siddim,
   full of slime pits. I dreamed
    that for seven days I should eat flowers only,
     that someone would come for me,
      that the gall of a fish
       would wipe the blindness from my father's eyes.

We would seek death, but not find it.

Azarias, as I knew him too, led me
 to my wife, and we lived fifteen years
  together before this voyage
   called me away to wander at the edge
    of everything -- psilocybin, bindweed,
     the white stone with the name of God
      caught inside, the indole alkaloids,
       the sea itself--

                    "And I took the little book
                    out of the angel's hand and ate
                    it up; and it was in my mouth
                    sweet as honey; and as soon as I
                    had eaten it my belly was bitter."

III

We have been becalmed a week,
 and wait for the wind
  at Sitia, in the east of Crete.
   I have amused myself with the local
    epic, the *Erotocritos* of Konarnos,
     lately dead.
       The Venetian governor is something
        of a scholar and connoisseur of wines,
         but I have done no business.
          We meet occasionally at the Crystal Hotel,
           speak, and go our way. He does not
            trust merchant sailors or Turks.
If the wind does not rise tomorrow
 I will go to the monastery at Toplou
  to trade for wool and mohair, melilote,
   ikons, and leather bags.

God would that I had one filled with wind!

I do not know how many years
 before I may return. So much depends
  on love, and the next port.
   My heart is hardly more than an odor
    driven outward by the wind, far past
     capturing. Not the storyteller,
      nor the acid memory of music
       can make it real again, and put it
        in my hand. Yet I must steer
         by it alone.

I would rather strip myself
 and bathe with oreads than know the Talmud,
  for the will is flesh
   and the diapason a flutter of water and lips.
    Blake and the honey bee, the orb weaver,
     the swallow, the dromedary, the mountains entire.
I feed my heart on him, his verse
 a "firm perswasion," and a secret homily
  to the woods, a tessellation of mystery,
   a language not to be interpreted but learnt.

Everywhere proportion and blessed madness,
 human light, the soft play of wind on flesh.
  If the eagle of Ezekiel tears at my heart
   as at the cedar of Lebanon,
    and I am enthralled to a covenant,
     I yet would have my seed grow in a forest
      where Blake was loved, the garden of Adonis
       thrived, and the Rose of Sharon walked.

I have had enough of dust,
 and the sea is a great weariness.
  I pine for home.

I want to go east no more.
 My name is Longjaunes, born in Tunis,
  and I have traveled too far.
   My wife waits in Málaga
    with my boys
     I sell Falernian wines, and many herbs:
              saffron, fenogreek, sesamum, colyrium,
              sarpangandha for insanity, buchu leaves,
              coca, betel nut, gambir, pennyroyal,
              and the five cinnamons.

I first went to India with Hippalus, later,
 still a youth, to China by the Silk Road,
  four times to the New World.
    Once, on the White Nile, as far
     as Malakal, where the great swamp begins.

Ergot will bring a baby out, though too much
 blackens the fingers
  in Saint Anthony's Fire.

I have the humor of Moses, and look
 at the ground when I walk, but I
  am hardy, and my father taught me
   useful trades.

The visions my father covered me with
 have formed my life, the healing music
  of herbs and simples,
    the wanderings, the refusals.

I wait at Sitia for the wind to blow,
 hungry for the sadness of love.
  I have gone as far along the coast
   as I can without getting killed.

I come from the woods or the sea, stumble
into a city and find delight
 in the things I dread -- gimcrack
  hawkers, saloons, taxi drivers,
   the broken clerks at Woolworth's,
    cooks, beggar boys, blind lepers,
     drunken carpenters, witches, a public
      execution, the open cafés.
I lose myself in the easy distractions
until the scent of a gillyflower
 or the odd wheeling of a gull
  sets me thinking of home.

Then I am lost again, and wonder
 what price I could get for my ships
  if the war were over.

At Málaga I would have orange groves
 and vineyards and grow a hillside of saffron,
  and keep one small ship for flight, or pleasure
   in North Africa.
    My wife would come to know my face again,
     and I would make the poems
      I lately only talk about.

Potency is a sleeping seed in a line of poetry,
  the defect impurity and intoxication
  -- an infant deer with tigers, a serpent
  hiding in a hollow bamboo
    age a leopard
    time a wolf
      death a white-faced horse
      hobbled beside an ant hill.
Always the moon-bliss of the Chakora bird.

The bliss of entering a woman,
  the idiot joy of the old Taoist madmen,
    the gibbering Kula-yogin, who
    laugh in seven voices and forever,
      playing hide-and-seek on the mountains.
      Getting out of the cold wind.
Gathering spikenard in Sikkim,
  the river howling five thousand feet below,
  the smell on your hands.
    The radical joy of the temple.
    And, which is the same, the humor
    of children.

            "Honey from the reed called sacchari"

Yes, Ornette Coleman's saxophone,
  absolute improvisation, the order
  of flux and breath, Cecil Taylor
    on piano: "I try to imitate
    the leaps in space
    a dancer makes."

Time is distance,
  or fingertips on nipples and keys.
   Finding the corners of the poem
    to tip it over
     to a new shape
                    . fold it
                    eat it
                    throw it in the air
run all the way home with it
 home when the wind rises
  the leaps in space a dancer makes.

My wife's face.

The chief corporal works
  of mercy are seven
    like the days: to feed the hungry
                      to give drink to the thirsty
                      to clothe the naked
                      to visit the imprisoned
                      to shelter the homeless
                      to visit the sick
                      to bury the dead.

I would teach a man to thresh,
 find his way in the woods,
  to whittle toys, make whisky
   and sew, to cherish
    books, to retreat before others.

Good boots, a knife, a sheepskin cloak
 are worth more than a passport,
  yet what does the fox know
   but the law?

Those who venerate the Zodiac
 today
  have never looked at the stars.

                    My mind wanders
                    though my element is fixed water
                    my number 4

The excellence of geography
lies in the clarity of its demands.
 Men are obscure, and devious,
  and to love a woman is more difficult
   than to traverse the desert of Lop
   alone.

Yet it is with a woman
 that ordinary men are tested.

                    "go along the coast as far as
                    you can without getting killed."

And come back.

The moon is only the first of the dead,
 and I sit with my face to the air,
  playing with strings, and watch
   the hills pick at the sky, caught
    in memory of a cave I lived in.
     Down the hill a bit there was a monastery,
      and the music from it was as good as wind.

The short, high notes of the thigh-bone trumpet,
the smoky, deep-bellied rasp of the cymbals,
the razz and rattle of human voices.
It was a little like New Orleans
but everybody drank buttered tea
and prayed.

I had six books and a round
mirror I could flash signals
to the peaks with, or look at,
and a fifth of straight malt Scotch.
Sundown I'd take a drink,
then maybe whistle for a while
or work on some new cat's cradles.

It's a mouthful to say goodby
in Tibetan. The first one says
"Kalechudenja," which means sit down slowly.
Then the other says "Kalechibgyunang,"
and that means go slowly; then they walk away.

The last is the hardest to say.

But I think the wind is rising.

from THE FIRE VISIONS

THE FIRE VISIONS

A line shack on Summit Ridge,
a coal-oil lamp, a kaleidoscope,
pocket Bible, Dumézil's *Légendes
sur les Nartes,* the terror
of cities carried by the wind.
Lived a week on oatmeal, raisins,
seven sticks of cinnamon for tea,
a lid of grass. The old prophets
circled the cabin like bears,
their pelts thick with fire,
holding apples in their hands
made into eyes.
The Nart born of a stone
howled each night like a knife blade
ripping at the stars.
The whirring cries of the Cedar
Waxwings were like wool
scarves of sound.

A year out of time, a pool
of agate and moss, the drift
of black sand that carries gold
as surely as a dream carries
unspent wishes.
I gathered the feathers
of a hawk God had brought down,
plaited them into my hair
and danced a wingless flight
above the canyon, the flames
like oboes and oranges.
Fire is an apple, and the poets
—psalms hanging from their necks,
full of the pleasing grace, wander
the forest clad in soft leather
with a bright knife at side,
a flute, a palm's-full of raisins.
A tree is an apple, and books
are lovely to hold as the flesh
of lovers, apples too.

Words are pinecones and acorn,
the brushy seed-cage of the larch,
hemlock's life in shade
and burn with the music Daniel made,
for whom dreams were pearls and mirrors,
who understood the substance of the fire.
The taste of fire is apples.

The poem tied to the cedar shingle
with the stub of a pencil,
Gabriel perched on the ridge-pole,
the rain outside hard as Noe's
third day, the birds afraid in the hold,
The poem spent curses sharp
as splinters, old wisdom pulsed
something more than a mystery: slice
into an apple and blood pours out,
rich as from a severed head, but
filled with such light
it may not be seen.

Buckskin is a soft fate,
and the femur of a doe
fits the haft of my knife blade
to my hand's content, the rasp
shaping it carefully as a stanza.

I would print my books on cedar
and with apple ink
and mix the wine in my triton
shell with gin: God speaks
to men clothed in feathered capes,
with hats of owl-skin, and masks
made of beaten copper
stolen from old graves.
Here on the rim I lean
against a Douglas Fir and stare
like a gambler beyond the book
into the air that packs the canyon.

MY COW

The stones rattle on the hillside
in the fog: the brindle cow is lost,
or drunk again on jimson weed.
she wants to fly, thinks
she is flying, but her hooves
run out of air deep in the heart.
She shakes her head like a dog,
and lows with long, dizzy notes
slipping from her throat, the white
depths groaning under the press of flowers.
She is dreaming, and clambering
toward the moon, or a sunrise
spliced into the night.
The light from her bones blinds her,
the soft edges of stone reach out
like bramble fingers, pluck at her ribs,
pinch her ears. She's speaking Chinese
now: "Wan wu chih mu" she bugles,
calling on The Mother to tame
the stones, melt the snow
that burns in her four bellies, get
her back to earth.

I follow two miles in the fog,
find her the lee side of a watertank
in soft repose, belching,
smiling like an old man.

TWO DAYS THE BUDDHA WIND WAS BLOWING
for Mary Ann

At Shrirangapatna I received
the sacraments of fire and water.
The flames passed underneath my hands
and my fingers caught the soot like cobwebs;
the water pressed in my cupped palms,
          and as I had seen others do,
I sipped
and streaked my forehead and my hair.

In the shadows behind the priest, black
and disconsolate, sated, bored by prayers,
stood a Name.

Because I am alien, and oblique,
and catch myself sliding out of mirrors,
I often stand where the edge of the river
meets the field of consciousness.
What have I to do with loss?
I pilfer my own memory for gestures.

Stones are capable of waiting out the night,
their conversation lapsed, like horses
standing decently apart in the corral,
vaguely worried about starlight
falling on their coats
and the threads of silver soldering their hooves
to earth.

The woman's smile of a moon,
blinding, wet as cream,
slides in luminescence on the fence posts.

Beyond that edge of air,
deep in the temple,
the Name is spelling Itself
to Itself, keeping us going,
letting the Buddha wind rise.

This acceptance by the heart of everything,
the dark figure on the river's bank
that dives and swims across
and disappears

            is all the Name remembers,
caught this time in sooty stone
shaped to Vishnu's body, the patient
object of prayers and flowers,
calm as a dreaming horse.

WITNESSING THE PHOENIX

Wind has its calm at center, in the flute's
bore, in the contemplations of Bernoulli.
When flames rattle heedlessly from wood,
its hardness swirled to gas, this is
the bird transforming itself, or old men
talking, the wind feeding its death
over a log.

You may not interfere with the burning,
only wander and look throughout your life.
Pilgrim, you may
speak if you know what to say.

The bird's screams rise like swarms
of bees. Immortality is harder to bear
than life.
Nothing you possess or understand
can tempt the bird; what you believe
are snakes convulsing in the dust
beneath the tree are that,
and you will find your feet move
independently as spiders. You
will dance.
And when the long bandage of fire
unwinds itself from his bones,
and the bird squalls like a baby,
his raw head dangling from his new-born neck,
yet tries to rush at the skies as avidly
as a rapist punches the crotch of his prey
--his mind burnt by other fires,
breath and heartbeat chained to him
like idiot brothers--
You know why wind has its calm at center,
in the flute's bore, why music ends.

SEVEN TEMPLES TO GOD IN THE AIR

The grey of the Sierras
granite, schist, clouds
gone hard in time
Junipers, live oak, madrone
   Tansy
      sexy tansy.
Don't read many poems
anymore
only the lives of the poets

"Warm in the hutch
of her escutcheon hair
his burning was his life"
&c.

Painting in the hand
of the painter: the walk
of a water ouzel through a stream.

I hold a pale flint arrowhead
to the light
and would swear
that there was a man
with his arms outstretched
hanging inside.

We are untouched, ghostly lovers
locked in the membrane of our skin,
in a bag of flesh and words--
Though we would have
at least a carnal knowledge
of philosophy.

Ajanta could have been in New
Mexico, the cut
and curve of the canyon,
the cover, places
around the Peñasco
or the Rio Feliz.

Ellora like Navaho country,
save that labor in the stone.
The Navaho walks
easy on rock, content
with the temple of the air.
Though the Kiva a
holy womb and a longing.
The cliff-carved temples
deserted and meaningless,
A poem the dance
of a man in his cell
his life.

                    Rimbaud at the R R station
                    Snyder on Suwa-no-se
                    Valéry addressing
                    the French Academy
                    Crane drunk
                    Vallejo hungry
                    Liddy, civilization,
                    talking
                    Lowenfels' beret.

Woman bathing
in the Bagmati River
her breasts bare

Surviving in
the greenest valley on earth
where a swollen-bellied
baby shat and the still
living shadow of a dog
lapped at the ground.

No scene too terrible
if those who have peace
must prepare for war.

And in the temples
as in the arrowhead
hangs a man.

The treasury of Meenakshi
Temple, gold and jewels
huge crack'd rubies
         in the face of so
         much beauty:
            The Sierras.

The soundness of whole stone
the cliff a temple
by which a climber adores
the heights
A theology of granite
the growing limestone
of the cave
Pure, with water.

> That remains pure
> which makes no decision,
> but those who would live
> must worship death.

A poet's life the revolution
The ancient serpent sucks his tail
the circle turns,
the water-ouzel clambers
swiftly through the stream.

LISTENING TO MAPS

The sounds of old maps
is like dolls' laughter,
brittle as china twigs
or a bird's thinking.

At Dodona, old men
still listen to the oak,
and yellow-eyed boys
have begun to dream at the signal
            of things shuffled in the night
since the stars were first seen,
and their names began to be understood.

The page is a mind's track.
Everything reveals. It is not necessary to read.
Wittgenstein is folded in the limestone
The whole of the mysteries
is held like music in the white bark pine.

Every ridge is sacred to a bird
who watches the river below
twist like a juniper with secrets.

What the maps don't tell me
I discover from my wife.
Love knows things denied all else.

Some maps can be rolled like waves,
while others have to be folded at the joints,
bent like canal locks, or opened up,
like shy girls' thighs.

Old maps demand the least,
like old men: they've learned
the fallacy of presumption,
and everything goes easier
with the eyes closed.

There is no way to satirize a map.
It keeps telling you where you are.
And if you're not there,
you're lost. Everything is reduced
to meaning.

A map may lie, but it never jokes.

We are sitting here, you and I,
in a place on a map.
We know this.
Yet we are not on the map.

We are looking for ourselves.
This is the rustle of leaves
that you hear,
the crackle of folding paper,
the sound of old maps.

THE RIM OF THE GREAT BASIN

Q. What is the holy power of the wilderness?
A. The holy power of the wilderness is innocence
   of man.
                              The Catechism

Darkness is another kind of light,
and stones are sweet as air to breathe.
The Anasazi, the old people, knew.
In the depths of canyons
for a thousand years, they unlocked
the rocks themselves and slipped
inside like bones fit into skin.
They watch as the bristlecone
pine signals from the ridge,
and know how flames leap from
flint and steel.
The bighorn desert sheep nests
like a bird above the falling land,
unseen by man, and mountain boomers
play their cylindric minds
on the silences which are wisdom.
Canopus hangs like a breathing eye
in the arms of the pine, and the long
interchange of their awareness
is the heart beating at the core of everything,
a music of smoke and crystal, an impenetrable
language shaped out of time and the graceful,
falling curve of space between them.

KAI

for Gary, Masa, and Kai

The deer pick their way
toward the fallen pears,
the child beckons to them,
their eyes are golden
leaves as they stare.
The child grows a starfish
in his mind, and bends its legs
into music that the deer
dance to.
The sweetness of fallen
pears is harmony, the deer
pick the fruit from the ground
though they have no hands,
and inside the child
rise the heavy shoulders
of Mount Kailas
and the impenetrable
blue waters of Manasarovar.
The deer drink at the lake.

THE ROCK CLIMBER

We are a carnival for the Lord.
He applauds like a dreaming fox,
full of the glory of His imagining
and the intemperate landscapes
of His dreams.
He believes our adventures.

I balance my life
on an ancient granite cliff
and He applauds again.
hoping I do not fall.
He is a good Lord,
and He loves us,
though He has made
the cliff like glass
and turned up the rain
to beating.

ONE

The theory is
memory prefigures the coming
reality of the past,
the dream reminds me
what I've done, or have to do:
on the hand, a ring,
the bezel showing a serpent
drinking from a cup.
In the shadows, a dead face
and a heart of string.

TWO

I do not know
what else can be loaded
into the mind.
But I want to remember
a time long enough ago
that the seas were fresh,
and faithful,
when lust had a sweet breath,
and learning wasn't much more
than a curiosity
to someone who was hungry
or lost in a woman.

THE HE-LINNET

A bull house finch at the feeder,
his body light and delicate
as a cracker. Somehow
a quarter-ounce of down
and brain got him through
the winter.

LITANY

Bless wife and children,
bless friends.
Bless whitening hair
and blurring sight,
bless heart's malaise.
Bless snow-blocked trails,
bless no escape,
bless black and fell despair.
Bless murder's empty face
and give it eyes.
Bless beer, bless dope,
bless dynamite.
Bless poems, bless art,
bless blessèd books.
Bless the wounded's sighs.
Bless night pulled
round my shoulders
like a shawl (or shroud).
Bless all.

METAPHYSICS

1955 lived with Dora
in a little shack up the valley
from El Paso.

gardened and had castor beans
12 feet high, a bed of nasturtiums.

Lady driving by stopped her car
and remarked on the castor beans,
saw the nasturtiums, thick blooming,
and told me
       "Nasturtiums don't grow here, you know."

What I don't know how to tell
is that I *like* people who can think that way,
and wished I could myself,

knowing the proper order
is elsewhere.

ONTOLOGY

Very little exists.
Chicago, for example
does not exist.
I have seen it twice
and there is nothing there.
It does not even have a history.

**

Grasshoppers do not exist
either.
Minute examination
reveals them as small
webs of colored light,
vibrating like stars.
Nothing more.

***

Old texts say
a few trees exist,
but they are so deeply
hidden in the woods
that it is unlikely
any will be discovered
in our day.

REPTILES

Lizards have small
leather hearts.
The eyes of newts
are balls of twine
wound tight.
Snakes are made
by braiding hair
in water, the child
snake gathers needles
for his teeth.
Dragons have no bones
and float like cobwebs
in the wind.
The salamander sleeps in fire,
in the warm odor
of wet moss and sulphur,
peeling skin.
Each tortoise carries
a single word
of the Qlippoth Kabbala
woven into his shell,
mounts stones at times,
in his mistaken love.

FOUR BIRDS

Bird I
Numenius phaeopus

The curlew pits my veins
with his footprints,
strolling through the chambers
of my heart like a sightseer
in a cathedral, picks
clots of doubt from the walls
with whimbrel grace, writes
nothing, breeds from Arctic
coasts south to Yukon Delta.

Bird II
Pica Pica

A nasal querulous maag? cry
while in hooping flight
like mortar shells, knowing
death is holy and good to eat,
links homo lupus to Magpie,
toe back, apposed thumb
—pollex or passerine
intelligence the same,
we live and speak together
at the side of the road,
our young also greenish, blotched,
   though magpies
      do not make war.

Bird III
Megaceryle alcyon

The Kingfisher rattles his bones
like pistons and gears, but he is
as shy as a titmouse and dies
if you shit in his waters.
Saw one way up the Palouse
five years ago, none since.
The waters warmer, browner.

Bird IV
Synthliboramphus antiquum

Low calls in the colony at night,
the Ancient Murrelet survives
at sea, the Pribilofs, Baja.
Stays in the open, away from
men, memorizing the old songs,
standing on the edge
of a thousand foot cliff
from which he tumbles in delight
at an image.

THE BEAR THAT CAME TO THE WEDDING
Epithalamium for Patte and Ralph 7 VI 69

In this poem the Bear shambles in
    like a slightly drunken uncle,
politely hands the Bride
    a tidy knot of Shooting Star, Strawberry
Blossoms, and Violets, nips
    the Groom gently on the left shank
and disappears, humming or snorting
    we are not sure, but dancing
certainly, and we are left alone
    with the enormity of the forest's blessing,
wondering what to make of our lives after this,
    the Bear's visit, thinking it might mean
                Love.

POPPIES

I am not sure what burns in my head
when I walk a long way, after whistling dims,
but this morning the enamel blue sun,
hot as an apple, sent me all of a sudden
poppy crazy—petals like feathers
or crêpe paper, and I slipped
from my body like spilled water.

Wandering, I have found stones
for my pockets as accurate in shape
as flutes or the bodies of insects,
yet when the sun circles overhead
like a lazy hawk, and my fingers
run on the tissue of petals, I feel
thin as a photograph, a vague emulsion
stripped from history.

I wear dark glasses and talk
to strangers in bars, telling them
I have wrestled with an angel
and been broken, that the god
of the winds is mad, and clothed in poppies,
though his fingers reveal
the huge power of ordinary things
when he speaks of the other redemption:
        enough blood to soften the flesh about a bone.
        enough consciousness to dodge a wasp.

THREE POEMS FROM CUSIK
AND NORTH SKOOKUM CREEK

1.

    A landscape like southwest China
    Stars through the fir and larch straight up
    Washing dishes in the dark, thinking
      of Li Shang-lin
        or someone in exile.

    You take the road to Usk.

                  **

2.

    The water, ya!
    cold
    and the laughter of friends.

                  **

3.

    Celia washing her hair—
    two trout
    watch from the pool.

HER DRUM

A drum creates language.
                    Each one.
And the chamois bags we carry
                    (bits of charcoal, blue glass beads,
                    pomegranate seeds, a basil leaf,
                    an old coin, a clove)
are the easiest mathematics we have.
"Beating the drum is a form of weaving"
Observe: the frost on cabbage leaves,
a sot, a dry ox, cock's runes, the left-handed
path of a wanderer, the marks left on stone
by the Nephilim.
"These redeem love," she told me,
"renounce study and preaching,
bring me the herbs of the Zodiac."
I went swimming upside down in dreams,
chewing on a cinnamon stick
and tasting whisky, watching
a jackal circle in the dark.
The drum, like the cinnamon stick,
is real, and the covenant stones
bruise head, heel, and butt.
The old men pelt me
to dance; I do, and she has only one more
ordinance: "Now you know who Nobodaddy's
                            momma is, eh?"
And I of coastlines, salal thickets, long words,
I, I nod O.K.

NOTES FROM A JOURNEY TO SHAMBALA

I went simply to find the source
of the Kalachakra Tantra.

The horizon is ever like a woman,
approachable.

The idea of limit comes with the sea,
witness the olive-breathed Greeks.
But in Central Asia only the limitless
is reasonable.

The wholesomeness of mountains

There is some trick in folding the map
so that the true geography is revealed.

For twenty-seven days I walked north
and slightly to the left.

There are four places beyond which
there is no water, no water at all.
The mountains ring you entirely.

Amne Machen, to the south.

I swam the Snake River last year,
the Oxus this.

Occasionally, smoothing the ground
for a fire, I would find carved stones.
In one camp, a dozen intricate birds.

Some canyons run for miles, their
walls so steep and polished water
won't bead
but
runs like thin blood.

There, the whole purpose of rain is defeated.

Some of the birds, perhaps carved
by the same master, flourish one tail feather
of contrasting stone, thin as rice paper,
slipped into a socket
like a tiny flying penis.

These have been chipped by time,
but I collect them, and have buried
forty-seven
at this week's waterhole.

WALKING TO THE FAR SEA

A Suite For Bear

Climbing high above Cedar Creek today,
the road just about gone, my ghost
darted from the car, slid into the thickets,
began a lean-to of logs, piled moss, ferns,
wild strawberries growing on the slant,
a fire-circle of rocks studded with calcite
and mica, the stream twenty feet away, a sound,
a glint through the leaves, lived there,
feasting on shadows, my songs silver as trout,
birds roasted with sorbapples.

At night the pulses of sleeping trees,
their dreams caverns and air, for they proceed us
into the earth, and scratch at the sky's back
in indolence. A tree is God with his slippers on.
Stories of a wildman, a woodwose matted with leaf
and hair, a logger chanced on him once
and he gibbered, fled, drooling shit from his backside,
a bird flying beside his head crying
sasquatch, sasquatch!
The bird either sits on the tree's shoulder,
or foot is caught there, and let go only out of humor.
I don't care. I don't need a manitou
to sleep in my hole. The tree hums at night.
It is afraid of fire.

I am becoming a bear. I roll in a bed of sage
at noon, and wrap my paws in the smell.
Hair is growing from the center of my palms.
The road is sliding down the hill.
Cedar Creek. Then Boulder Creek.
The car protects us. I will let the fire go out.
The forest is a language of long green tongues
more ancient than bears, and skillful.
Beyond the forest is the sea.

II

The last day
there is no tragedy, no conflict.
It is all here. Nothing
is missing.
One, and strong.
Walking.

The song is always given, never made.
As deer gives himself to us
when the time comes, and as we give.
For how else can we stay alive?
The ancestors dream us
and we are, growing out of the soil.

The word for life is daylight,
and a man who can call up bear
is strong beyond us, a man
who could breed mules in Elis.

A serpent hangs from the sky
with his head over the sea.
He is swaying his head to and fro
and singing.

III

A dream toward morning: words
snapped from the mouth like teeth,
thrown as birdshot. You put
them to sense, the sun shining
between your legs.
Cogito, but cannot say why; *sum*
but will not add.
Rather subtract my eyes
Numb-er fingers to decide
truth. Claws

5 is. Circuitous ways
their search leads to the hills
or the sea
Tongue full of maggots
all whispering "hold to the pebble"
   "these are the flowers of Africa"
   "a dry soul is wisest and best"
"taste the tenatsali"
"it is all evasion"

A furlong against a hundred fathoms
to the west, the bell
of the sea
crying like a woman.

IV

Descent into birth, the forest.
I don't know what we suffer from!
The shadows puff and bark like dogs
at murder, the foul breaths of spirits burn,
light blows through the waves in webs of smoke,
the trees afire.

                      I slip into the nightdress of the sea.
Blind, eyes torn by the beak of God
who is an owl, I had endured
the labor of these dreams till my bones
were the laughter of cedar
and mind was all the bear's—neutral
and moving through the forest
as easily as a hand runs through hair.
                 At a certain depth the water ends
and a long cave of greasy air works down
to center (once breaking through I caught
my chin and shoulder in the membrane
and hung gibbeted above the dark, again
a strangled child, till I broke free
and fell like Blake between Saturn
and the fixèd stars).

Father, the agility of our wrath
ends intelligence, and what I do—
ill, fevered, head full of broken words,
my paws burning and wet,
is made wholly my own by our dispossession.

Mouths made of skin tell me to to live,
but there are creatures here inside
whose names alone will kill,
who speak no transformatory prayer,
who know my scent.

SPIRITUAL EXERCISES

Two nights before Christmas
and I'm making a vajra-stick
out of white pine
scraps
a Nepalese rig
blast out a mountain
in the solid hells
if you get it there
otherwise make
Mother Padma-Krotishaurima
choke

                  through terror and awe

                  through terror and awe

on the blood she carries
in a shell

Now it entertains the kids
who wave it in the air
like a sword or butterfly

and know purely

                  "Even at the time
                  that the pebbles
                  are being counted out,
                  be not frightened,
                  nor terrified;
                  tell no lies;
                  and fear not
                  the Lord of Death"

that it will float
like a kite
in the sea.

EARLY POEMS: 1955-1965

from PRECISE FRAGMENTS
      12 BONES
      THE SPANISH DARK

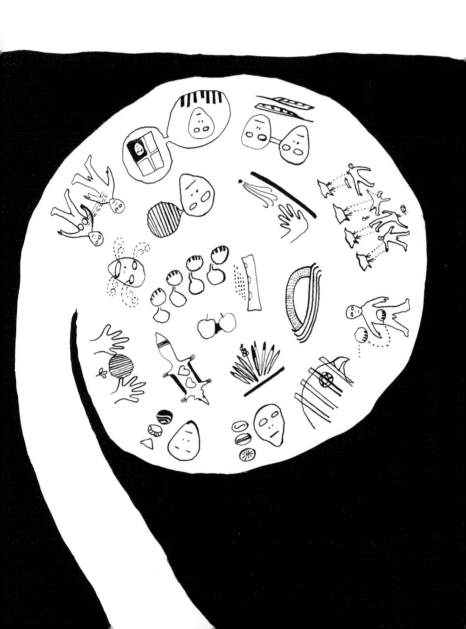

SONG

All I want for Christmas (Michaelmas will do)
Is a curling stick, two apples, half a shoe
(To fit the mind my thought is footed to).
For Hilary or Trinity (Whitsuntide will do)
I want a golden pear, black music from a flute,
A unicorn, and you.

SZE CHUAN: 1929

The helmsman's hands have washed
The tiller's grain to marriage.
His palm is teak,
The tiller's sheen is flesh.
And half the rain that fills
The gorge on which we float
Ran off his back last year.

THE VOICES OF ROCKS

Rocks speak in the small voices of insects,
Dry chitterings that complain the heat
And dust and trod of man. So soft
They are drowned by the brass
Rubbing of leaves and the string-
Tense strain of wind bent branches.

When wet they mumble of the mud
And flood the rain pocked streets
With the flow from their shoulders
And wound cats' ears with cries
Pitched higher than a shriek
Of mole claw caught and torn
From grass.

They never sing.

COLLEAGUE

A young professor, scholarly
And a little distant, showed
Me a private treasure from his wallet.
The wings of a moth
Inexpensively laminated
Between plastic sheets.

One odd night the insect
Perched on his wife's brow
And he caught it easily.
His fingers tremble slightly
As they point to the wings' design:
Hebrew letters, he says, spelling
Out his name and God's.

MEN AND WOMEN

Fine hairline cracks, mild concussions,
Chips, greenstick fractures,
All are, if not enlightening, at least
Productive of the suffering
By which we can be redeemed.

It is not possible to believe this
Unless one has been lost
And burnt on the hope of being found.
It is not possible to believe this
Unless one has hung like a dried fox
On the fence of somebody's love.

THE SPANISH DARK

I

Books for rocks now fifteen years
and they'll do for poor man's stone,
but do not ring
do not make that fundamental grunt
when you rap them together.
I have felt bone and skin and feathers,
singing in my fingers at the textures
always a code
a message.

The Spanish contours, the boundaries,
the Indian of my bowels sings to the ground
feels sex for rocks and the one-eye sun
knocking splinters of heat in my head.
On the far canyon side a wild ass
going on ground he knew, the ocotillo
and yucca the potent anxiety of the land.
I have sat out a winter wind
with my back sucking at the little heat
the wall gave and the sun thin and whining
beyond the overcast.

I have not been lost in the desert,
but by the axe, the bow, the smooth pebble.
The knife, the arrow, the sling.
And helpless before a plow.
I cannot kill. I have not
been that hungry.
The white man kills very well
and I notice the wild ass.

When I plant seeds sometimes they come up.
I watch them carefully and pat the ground
at their roots for message.
I am willing to carry water for a few plants
but I am better herding goats.

And the Spaniard?
One walked eight years in my country
seeing without Indian eyes the crucifying
thorn, the rocks that work penance
into the feet, the water promised tomorrow
and the food two days more.
The ignorance of the Spaniard.
The armor, the heaving horses,
the monks sweating in habits,
the naive vision of conquest.
The existence of truth, the possession
of the ego. The nakedness of the lost one.
The on walked the desert at night, the wild things close by.

Additionally there is the Spanish Dagger.

Cactus
twelve inches hawse-rough fiber pointed
with the hint of yellow venom inside.
Right through a boot.
Get one in the calf and it aches.
You've moved the point around inside
somehow and there is a bruise meshing
with the puncture. The poison made
my knee joint ache. I was chill
and hurting and I wanted to stop
and hug myself into my past.
The Spaniards, too.

I was born a Mexican in space
but not in time, as the Bostonian
is born an Englishman in space
but not in time. The land is Mexico,
the border is a delusion of the whites.
The sand belongs to both sides of the river;
it blows back and forth, back and forth.
Everybody born in the drainage of the Rio Grande
is an Indian or a Mexican.

After the Spanish conquered it they
turned into Mexicans. The land wins.
The Indian wins.
Because the Mexicans turn into Indians
if they live in the land.
The land only loves Indians
who plant it easy and pat the ground
to call the water down the row
and it comes licking along the corn stalks
like a puppy.

III

The Apache drug, Cofradia in the water-fist,
the brotherhood of dark, the night cowl.
Narcosis of the desert hangs in the black,
clasp in stones, and in the solid thorns burn issues
and the final demolition of wisdom.
I agree to the loneliness,
refuse to ignore the interiors, the spaces,
the web-clefts, the bacon spiders.

The blue enamel cup warms my hands
in the desert of Soete
and the tan drink throws
out fans of steam. Hunkered,
back to the wind, Levi collar stiff on my cheek,
I wait for
He will bring it.

Lying beneath the mesquite
I convulse slowly, the body
rubbing at the sand, the face
and eyes *risus*, the spine
hauled back, blocked in contraction.
The house has been entered.
This is the other canyon.
The emotions are piled at my left
like cheap dishes.
Knowledges were eaten there.

The action of the legs has pushed
the body into the mesquite.
A thorn catches my eyelid
and the sand grains are prisms
breaking the light into minds.
The minds speak the secrets.
                    The languages—
Lips move as fingers saying
roughly the Sumerian Gestalt,

the articulate swans, the mesalliance
of sanity and truth, the present brown
thorn holding my face.
The heave of the loins that is strangled
to a hunched thrust, the intention that
bones shall orgasm, that the burst
will be final.

The waters are deep over Cofradia
and the dreams burn in the waters,
settling to the depths that agony
is understanding. The pain is misinterpreted.
The pain is a disguise: it is a vestment
covering the release. Vanquished
by the spasm, the entering shadows of the minds.
What the language constructs
is nothing to the juice of voices, the speaking.

The adoption, the avowal that identity
is determined, is created, that the names
of flesh are given them in their crucifixion:
the hurt of density.
To be pushed and swollen together with such force—
here in the mesquite my brain is pulped by the massive
hands of the Apache. The liquid runs between
his fingers; gathered and crushed, a ball
of grass wiping the stains of meaning.
Discarded. I live mindlessly.
I have been backed into the interior of stone,
I have collapsed into crystal: the mind
now receiving only itself, reflecting
the blue rays backwards.

This is the flowing in the other canyon.
The world is in retreat before the inner surfaces,
the race across the lower surface.

The waters are mine to understand by possession.
The crystal heals.
The reward is to be a source,
to become geographical.

CONCERNING THE FERVID CARNAL ART

I should call it a secretion—A.E.Housman

Stepped in the aitch-bone,
The poem is a shaft hewn through flesh,
A country, the tunnel left by a star
(or a bird's death) and comes
Out the eyes and mouth
Hemorrhage.

A thick and palpable noise,
The poem is the node of a whistle,
Fixed and northern,
And we spin into tomorrow on it.

We shall
Pray and bleed poems
And kiss them like a face.

TAUGHT THE LANGUAGE

The Apache is my master,
the maker of word-cliffs
brown and freshlet,
wet galena crystal
dark and fat—
all his rudd garnet of syntax.

I am the deer says
the paradigm
and my tongue is man's hand
twisting the herbs
into a sweet ball.

FROM THE MINOR GNOSTIC PREACHMENTS

What drug will carry you to paradise?
What poem?

Even suicide brings you back
to stand mute and hurting
as a tree or lintel, a wagon-tongue.
Idiot leather perhaps, or a geographer's
skull-cap.

I myself am shoes.

We are to be broken,
or burnt.

Some of us are words that for a second
hang in the air and then evaporate.

Poems have long been smoke.

There is immersion in a discipline—
    the pattern of game in chess
    or mathematics
    or maybe love.

But out of nothing: that's the weakness
of games.
They are not connected to the skin.

But the skin language of love? (D.)
Simple.
Skin is shed.

THE OBJECTS AND CATEGORIES

Obsidian, chalcedony, flint:
the stones of the dead.

Tourmaline, jasper, and opal:
the stones of the living.

The herbs of the living
are tarragon, cumin, and rose.

The herbs of the dead
are pepper, oregano, and tar.

POEM AND MOSAIC FOR SARGIS TMOGVELI

Riding from the southwest
One sees the faces: carved
Stones set in the cliffs
Beyond the reach of waves.

The son of Barabbas cut
Them from the rock, working
Out the secret tremor
Of his hands.

"These are obscure people,"
He muttered, resting the point
Of his chisel in an eye-
Socket, "whose history has gone
Askew. And I am son of him
Chosen before God."

The surprise has become
A permanent part of his face.

Below, on the sea-trail,
Traders of Azerbaijan
(where the earth itself
Is thick with fire)
Carry wax and honey
And thick pads of fur.

They are dressed in Greek
Brocade and sweep past
The clamor of his work
Talking of the horse-shoes
Of Genje, the white falcon
In the boxwood cage, hazel-
Nuts that fetch wine
And Tibetan musk, ink-horns
Of Saman aloe.

> "We are all travellers,"
> He shouts from the cage
> His noise makes, but below
> The merchants speak
> Of Indian steel, Macedonian
> Locks, and the jewel
> Cut in the form of an anvil.

THE FIVE BROKEN STORIES OF A POOR MAN

1. When Alfred is three parts
   Gone from hunger,
   What is respect for the cornfield?
   A rock belongs to the man it hits.

2. We need not observe the untidy
   Attention that the owl pays
   To the obligation of the mouse
   To believe.

3. When the hull is dry
   The oakum lints out.
   So go aground.
   In a forest of spars
   Wedged and heaving
   Cables sweat and snap.
   The sea hides more mistakes
   Than the land.

4. Burn your plows
   And do not relax before flowers.
   They too are enemies
   And would deny their wilting.

5. All that the future provides
   Is a bindlestiff dream:
   And we have to give
   Everything for it.
   So we are who we have been
   What's that to tomorrow?

THE PAINTING

(for R.S.)

The hard disc of a Mexican sun
Drives into the canvas
As suddenly as an axe sinks into oak
And as cruelly as the thought of death
Tempts at the maimed.
Flowers are crushed and tattered
With the flat of a blade,
The spectrum is shredded, the pigments
Sing in cadenzas of danger,
For this has been a sacrifice.

The cadence is religious,
The colors swarm like hot bees
On the kernel of God,
And the shapes are the sounds
Of his signatures in time.

FOR DORA

We have had the years
To clarify our love—
That binomial expansion
Of self that lets us see
Of what the other's made.

Our success is not
That our virtues over-ride
Our faults, but that we're uncertain
Whose is which.

Best theory is that private
Persons met in marriage keep
All themselves that can be spared
From love, but this is none.
And so the paradox is begun,
And the dancing goes
Until the dancing's done.

WORK

If sweat has a sound
It must come from thin
Brass pipes, green
And pitted
Reminiscent of an experimental
Radiator.

Or the sound of breath
Through the teeth
Spittle
Shreds of air

And the sexual
Knotting
Of muscles.

FROM A GEORGIAN SHARD

Birds have teeth tiny as wisdom
And their nests are woven by captive Turks
And guarded by porcelain dogs
Stolen from a Chinese tomb.
In gatherings and clusters
They punctuate the air
And legislate the fate of trees.
Their power over man
Is limited to death,
Though their legs are thin
And their minds wind-swift
In evil.

POET AT WAR

haec perpetua mundi dementia est—Calvin

He rode the mule that brayed
At Appomattox: he broke pillows
On the faces of the dead
That they might have the softness
Of feathers.
Their eyes hid in the shadow
Of his idiot love.
He deciphered the clouds
For the dying and pulled laughter
From their mouths with the rocks
That would mate
At his single, piercing shout.

EQUIPMENT

Time and Sex:
Two heavy leaden
Ornaments attached to my body
By fishhooks.

Suits do not fit
Over them
And they
Clank when I walk.

Their presence is
Painfully
Obvious.

I ignore one
And the other
Ignores
Me.

Precisely the opposite
Of my desires.

Additionally
There is the knowledge
That we are being
Cheated.

LINES FOR UNAMUNO

et horror magnus et tenebrosus invasit eum
— *Gen. 15:12b*

Terror is not a taxed commodity,
Nor is it in short supply.
The future includes it.

Is it credible insight
To know that there is always
Somebody in the ruins?

No.

And that we should not remember
Who we have been, nor
Who we are, is natural.
Our condition makes the information
Negligible.

TRUTH NINE

Imagine that you push your head
Inside a rock
And turn on the light.
What would you see?

        Long lines of naked women
        Standing patiently to take
        A turn at the one
        Small
        Window.

TRANSLATION FROM THE PERSIAN

How happy the curses
From your cruel lips,
How elegant the milk
From your breasts.

You'll die of me,
Lovely,
If you don't live me
To death.

I give you a saying:

> Bread and onions with you;
> And years afterward, Troy burns.

A puzzle, eh?

THE BEACH OF ALTATA

What are the false virginities?
Silence, the night, the single Jew
In the Sabbath of the imagination,
A good serge suit of fear.

The frequencies of Nimue
In the forest of begettings
Where in sheaves of movement
David dances for the restoration
Of the Ark.

There each is in his proper pain.

    Littoral dream, the sand
    Loose and heavy underfoot,
    The mindless snipe
    Bleating at the waves,
    And men combing their horses'
    Coats beside the sea.

TALK

Sitting on the floor
two weeks ago
rum or whiskey by
that time thick
in the mouth
I spoke of sin
to a good woman
beside me

she laughed
and raised her drink
and I leaned my head
against her thigh

it was hard as
a mile runner's.

PISGAH SAYINGS

The critic who is not a prophet
is a dog.

The scholar who does not have a learned heart
is a cipher.

The poet who does not love
is a wind-reft fart.

TZJRA'S LETTER

I am not a whiteman.
I am an Indian—no more
from my tribe.
My name is Tzjra—which
doesn't mean anything.
It is only a pleasing sound
like John or Robert
or Alexander.

I have nearly forgotten how
to speak my language,
for there is no one left
Jalatz, my wife, died
ten years ago.
We spoke together
and waited for time to pass.

The irony of our situation
amused us, because we felt
like effete Romans at
the approach of the barbarian.
The people who replaced us
had little to commend them
save vitality.

They lacked any appreciation
of the incongruous.

We posed willingly enough
for the photographers.
—a certain minor sanity
in adaptation, perhaps—
And we refused them entrance
to our house—as they
expected.
We saw no reason to disappoint them.

It is romantic enough
being the last of anything:
But there is the danger
of dwelling too much
on the nothingness that
follows you. And thus
exaggerating the amplitude
of your present being.

Better to think that nothing
quite like us
will follow any of us.
For often no more distinguishes
Us but that we each
are unique—
The last of our kind.

I have claim to neither
wisdom nor property;
truth has been as shy of me
as money.
And I am sad that I never
regretted this.
A man should want truth, anyway.

But I have been content
with falsehood, dream,
illusion—all the humbug
that the whiteman
found amusing.
I should not put
the blame so—I found
it amusing as well.

Whitemen killed my grandfather
but no one has ever taken a shot
at me.
Nor have I given cause.
What was stolen is gone.
Our claim was no more than a wind.
For a moment, the wind covers everything.
Then it dies.

The whiteman's wind will die.
This is called history—
the last refuge of the defeated.

I think that to be
even a negligible human being
requires God's grace.
Some whitemen think this
but I did not learn it from them.
It is simply apparent.

And even an Indian
is permitted
the apparent.

BIBLIOGRAPHY

BOOKS & PAMPHLETS:

FRIEND, New Rivers Press, 1974.
MIRRORS, with drawings by Cheryl Doering, Stone Marrow Press, 1973.
THE DIARY OF A YOUNG GIRL, Lillabulero Press, 1972.
MAPS, with illustrations by Robert Sterling, Kayak Books, 1971.
GNOMONOLOGY: A HANDBOOK OF SYSTEMS, Sand Dollar Press, 1971.
SOME NOTES TO GARY SNYDER'S *MYTHS & TEXTS*, Sand Dollar Press, 1971.
OVENS: POEMS ON THE WAR AND TYRANNY, Black Rabbit Press, 1971.
THE FIRE VISIONS, Twowindows Press, 1970.
THE LIFE OF FRAENKEL'S DEATH (with Walter Lowenfels), Washington State University Press, 1970.
LONGJAUNES HIS PERIPLUS, with illustrations by George Nama, Kayak Books, 1968.
FABLES AND TRANSFIGURATIONS, Kayak Books, 1967.
THE SPANISH DARK AND OTHER POEMS, Washington State University Press, 1965.
12 BONES, The Goosetree Press, 1964.
PRECISE FRAGMENTS, The Dolmen Press, 1963.

FORTHCOMING:

CUTTING SIGN: Poems, 1971-1974.
THE PILGRIM'S TALE
DESERT
THE OLD BEAST

STORIES:

"The Great Toad Hunt," ARENA (Ireland), no. 4, Spring 1965.
"The Life of Battleship Billy," WESTERN HUMANITIES REVIEW, Fall, 1965.
"The Layman's Guide to Castration," THE GOODLY CO., no. 4, December, 1965.
"The Brigadier and The Nephew," THE GOODLY CO., no. 12, June 1968.

ESSAYS:

"Metcalf: The Sailings," LILLABULERO 12/13, Fall 1972.
"The Common Exile, The Single Ground," TO FIND SOMETHING NEW, Henry Grosshans, editor, Washington State University Press, 1969.
"The Wisdom of Silenus: Myth in the Modern World," UNIVERSITY OF PORTLAND REVIEW, Fall 1965.
"To The Death of Art," LALIT KALA CONTEMORARY (India), Spring 1967.
"The Vision of Rumplestiltskin," TRACE, no. 61, Summer 1966.
"The Arctic Desert," (an excerpt from Section One), STOOGE, no. 9, Spring 1974.